Marquis de Sade
meets Goody Two-Shoes

RONALD SEARLE

Marquis de Sade
meets Goody Two-Shoes

A FEW CROSSED PATHS & TREASURED MOMENTS

PAVILION

First published in Great Britain in 1994 by
PAVILION BOOKS LIMITED
26 Upper Ground, London SE1 9PD

The majority of the drawings in this book were first published
by the *New Yorker* magazine

Designed by Bet Ayer

ISBN 1 85793 466 0

Printed and bound in Great Britain by
Butler and Tanner Ltd, Frome and London

2 4 6 8 10 9 7 5 3 1

This book may be ordered by post direct from the publisher.
Please contact the Marketing Department.
But try your bookshop first.

INTRODUCTION

The theme of this collection, that of crossing a few unlikely paths, first emerged a year or two back, while I was re-dipping into the murky life of Edgar Allan Poe and re-encountering, that same afternoon, some of the worst of E. Hemingway's macho prose. Suddenly I had this distressing vision of Hemingway blasting the brains out of Poe's quothing raven, so that nevermore would the gloomy bird go on about doom, fate and the shocking price of bird seed in New York. From then on it was only a short trot to other fanciful encounters. Donatien Alphonse François, Marquis de Sade, for example. His sheer bad luck in crossing the path of the unspeakable Goody Two-Shoes, who was capable of crushing the spirit of men more monstrous and certainly less readable than he, was startling, to say the least of it. Is it not likely that one such numbing encounter – with or without skipping-rope – resulted in his incarceration and, finally, death in the lunatic asylum at Charenton? Such unlikely pairing opened up a world of nightmarish possibilities. Take old Omar Khayyám's brief encounter while he was lolling about with a loaf, a jug of wine and his girlfriend Thou, under a desert palm. If only he had enrolled in the Charles Atlas Biceps Course *before* T. E. Lawrence kicked sand in his face, the *Rubáiyát* might have been less soppy.

Crossed paths, like crossed legs, can conceal an awful lot of surprises. Had impetuous Caesar, for example, listened more carefully, would he still have chopped de Gaulle into three parts?

Well, maybe . . .

Robinson Crusoe meets Man Sundae

Gertrude Stein meets Spectre de la Rose

Edward Lear meets the Douanier Rousseau

Krazy Kat meets Mickey Mouse

Edgar Allan Poe meets Hemingway

Omar Khayyám meets Lawrence of Arabia

Arcimboldo meets Mrs Beeton

Little Red Riding Hood meets Beowulf

Freud meets Hieronymus Bosch

B.Traven meets the Invisible Man

Manet meets Nana

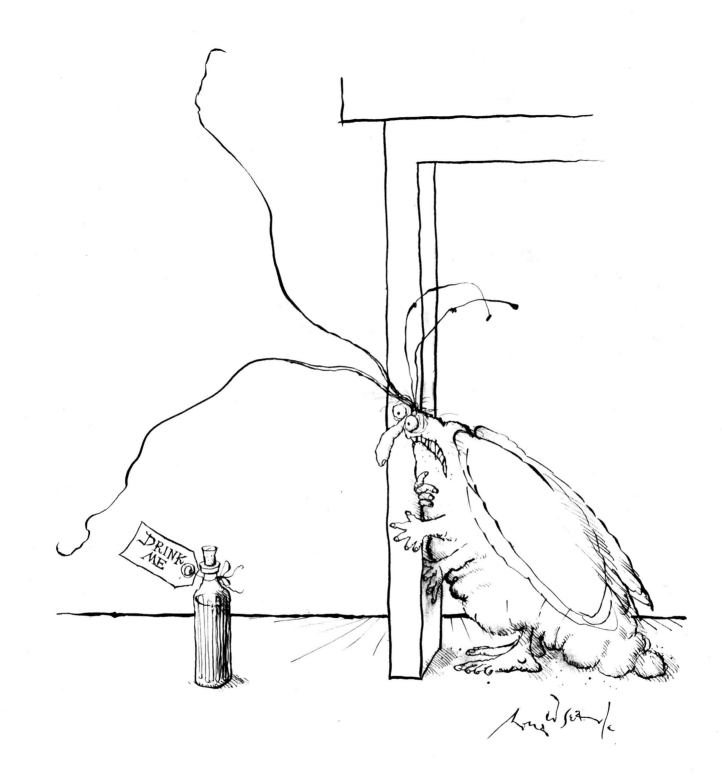

Kafka meets Lewis Carroll

Sleeping Beauty meets Rip van Winkle

Boswell meets Andy Warhol

Paris meets the Brontë sisters

Tom Wolfe meets the Tailor of Gloucester

The Hound of the Baskervilles meets Lassie

Marquis de Sade meets Goody Two-Shoes

Beethoven meets Munch

Samuel Pepys meets Richard Nixon

Rembrandt meets Thurber

Seurat meets Pasteur

Toulouse-Lautrec meets Don Quixote

Magritte meets William Tell

Count Dracula meets Boudin

Gargantua meets Jane Fonda

The Frog Prince meets Brillat-Savarin

Daisy Ashford meets Concise Oxford

Ford meets Sherman

Manet meets Josef von Sternberg

Kafka meets the Beatles

Isaac Newton meets Big Apple

Botticelli meets Busby Berkeley

Toscanini meets Chagall

De Gaulle meets Caesar

Icarus meets the Ancient Mariner

Izaak Walton meets Géricault

Monet meets Diamond Lily

Giacometti meets Olive Oyl

Little Bo-Peep meets Ulysses

Dali meets Narcissus

Oscar Wilde meets John Gay

Nietzsche meets Woody Allen

Mishima meets Vincent van Gogh

Laughing Cavalier meets the Cheshire Cat

Babar meets Hannibal

Whistler meets Mother Goose

Baron von Munchausen meets P.T. Barnum

RONALD SEARLE, creator of the St Trinian's girls and co-father of Nigel Molesworth, the Curse of St Custards, studied at the Cambridge School of Art. Since then he has contributed non-stop to a host of publications in Europe and America, particularly the *NewYork Times* and the *New Yorker* magazine, in which most of the drawings in this book appeared.

Also available from Pavilion Books:

THE CURSE OF ST TRINIAN'S
This spine-chilling collection of visual highlights from Searle's harrowing dossier is more relevant than ever, and is as painfully hilarious to parents and pupils as when they first appeared.

DOWN WITH SKOOL!
Nigel Molesworth, schoolboy philosopher, slayer of sentiment and ultimate survivor of the trials of skool and grown-ups breaks into print, with his masterly prose, cynical attitude and outrageous spelling.

HOW TO BE TOPP
From the maturity of one year's experience, Nigel Molesworth offers advice on how to survive french and latin, criket and foopball, how to be topp without doing any work, how to akquire culture and, above all, how to cope with bulies, snekes and grown-ups.

WHIZZ FOR ATOMMS
Molesworth's devices for dealing with the future, in this up-to-the minute guide to surviving modern life, include a production line for Latin sentences, a master-meter and the Molesworth-Peason electronick brane Mark VI for multiplication and division.

BACK IN THE JUG AGANE
Sentenced to another term at the deadly St Custard's, Nigel Molesworth rides again, dispensing wisdom and advice on teachers, examms, ko-eddukation, tenis, grown-ups (again) and – for the first time –gurls.

THE COMPLEET MOLESWORTH
Nigel Molesworth regales the reader with his own brand of lowdown on swots, snekes, swankpots, beaks, dirty roters, kanes, weeds and other chizzes in this classic of English humour. Introduction by Sir Tim Rice.